The
Interceding
Christian

The Interceding Christian

Kenneth E. Hagin

Unless otherwise indicated, all Scripture quotations in this volume are from the *King James Version* of the Bible.

Fifth Edition
Seventh Printing 2000

ISBN 0-89276-030-3

In the U.S. write:
Kenneth Hagin Ministries
P.O. Box 50126
Tulsa, OK 74150-0126

In Canada write:
Kenneth Hagin Ministries
P.O. Box 335, Station D
Etobicoke (Toronto), Ontario
Canada, M9A 4X3

Contents

1. Interceding for a Nation.......1

2. Dealing With Strongholds..25

3. Praying With the
   Help of the Holy Spirit.......43

Chapter 1
Interceding for a Nation

I exhort therefore, that, first of all, supplications, prayers, intercessions, and giving of thanks, be made for all men;

For kings, and for all that are in authority; that we may lead a quiet and peaceable life in all godliness and honesty.

For this is good and acceptable in the sight of God our Saviour;

Who will have all men to be saved, and to come unto the knowledge of the truth.

— 1 Timothy 2:1-4

In beginning our study on intercessory prayer, notice the word "first" in the scripture we just quoted. Things work when we follow directions; therefore, we want to take the Bible literally and do exactly as it says.

Too many times we say we believe in prayer and let it go at that. You could say you believe in driving an automobile, but that doesn't mean you can drive one. You could learn a lot by studying a handbook on driving, but there are some things you never would learn until you got in an automobile and started driving. You learn by experience.

Paul said in our opening scripture, *"I exhort therefore, that, FIRST . . . ."* Let's put first things first. Sometimes we let secondary things predominate, and neglect things that should be first.

In our spiritual life we blame God for our failures. We wonder why certain things don't go right, when, really, we are not putting first things first. Usually, people are putting themselves first, even when it comes to praying. But the Bible doesn't teach that. Many times prayers are not answered for you because you are putting yourself first.

Too many times people are like the farmer who prayed, "Lord, bless me and my wife, my son, John, and his wife — us four and no more." We may not put it exactly in those words, but that's the extent of our praying much of the time.

Paul said in our opening scripture that before we pray for ourselves or our families we should pray, *"For kings, and for all that are in authority. . . ."* That means we are to pray for our government — for those who are in authority — from the national level down to the local level. A few of us may be doing this now, but not many. If Christians were praying for our leaders, things would not be as they are in our nation.

Paul wrote under the anointing of God's Spirit, which means these words in First Timothy are God's words. God is not going to tell us to pray for something He's not going to give us. No father would tell his child he was going to buy her a doll for her birthday and then not do it. Certainly our Heavenly Father is not less faithful in His promises than an earthly father would be. God is not a man that He should lie. He will do what He says — when we meet *His* conditions. So many times there are *conditions* to be met in connection with prayer.

"I exhort therefore, that, first of all, supplications, prayers, intercessions, and giving of thanks, be made for all men; For

kings . . ." (vv. 1,2). In the time in which Paul wrote this, most countries had kings for leaders. Today's equivalent in our country would be our President. Paul then said, *". . . for all that are in authority. . ."* (v. 2). That means all our leaders — congressmen, senators, governors, mayors — *all* who are in authority. It even includes policemen.

It's so easy to criticize. I hear people criticize and I know they are not praying for our leaders; for when we pray for others we are not so apt to criticize them.

As Christians, however, we are not to put politics before Christ. Some people are so politically minded they are no good spiritually.

One time, for example, some political leaders in one section of the country were under criminal indictment. Later on they eventually were convicted and even sent to the penitentiary. But I overheard some Christians say they were going to vote for these men anyway. They didn't care if they had stolen two or three thousand dollars. They were going to vote for them because they were of their particular political persuasion, and they vehemently declared that one ought to vote a straight party ticket. It didn't make any difference who the candidates were. Fortunately, these politicians didn't get reelected.

There are some people who, if they did pray for someone who was not a member of their political party, would pray for him to be defeated. If the person were already in office, they would pray that he wouldn't be successful. That is a selfish prayer, and one that won't be heard or answered.

The Lord has impressed upon me that we should pray especially for our nation, for things can be changed through prayer. God doesn't tell us to do something just to put extra words in the Bible, or to fill up space. He has a purpose in mind. In our Scripture text we can learn the purpose of praying for our leaders.

Paul said to pray for those who are in authority so that we who are Christians *"may lead a quiet and peaceable life in all godliness and honesty"* (v. 2). God is concerned about us and will move, even though those who are in authority may not be Christians. He will answer our prayers and do things for us that we *". . . may lead a quiet and peaceable life. . . ."*

Notice the ultimate purpose of our praying for our nation. *"For this is good and acceptable in the sight of God our Saviour"* (v. 3). If we, as Christians, want to please God, what are we going to put as number one on our prayer list? Us? Our Children? Our grandchildren? Our church? No. We are going to do exactly as God said to do: pray *first* for all who are in authority.

Notice verse four: "*Who will have all men to be saved, and to come unto the knowledge of the truth.*" God's ultimate purpose in having us pray for those in authority is that we will be able to spread the Gospel. If we do not have good government where there is quietness and peace, it hinders the spreading of the Gospel. In times of political upheaval, we are hindered in spreading the Gospel. In times of war, we are hindered in spreading the Gospel, due to travel restrictions and other limitations.

God wants us to get the Gospel out. He wants us to get the truth out. Jesus said when He was here on earth, "*And this gospel of the kingdom shall be preached in all the world for a witness unto all nations; and then shall the end come"* (Matt. 24:14). The devil would do his best to see that this is not accomplished.

Ministers who have traveled extensively in other countries in gospel work tell me that while other countries are doing a certain amount of missionary work, America is about the only one carrying the Gospel to the world. Naturally, we see why the devil would oppose our nation so he could stop the flow of truth to the whole world. And we can see why God wants us to pray for those in authority, because He would have *"all men to be saved, and to come unto the knowledge of the truth"* (v. 4).

Now that we see *why* He told us to pray for our nation, let's look into the matter of how to pray for our nation. The scripture is clear

enough about *who* we are to pray
for when it says, *"For kings, and
for all that are in authority. . ."* (v.
2). But let's talk a little about the
how. Notice that Paul said,
*". . . supplications, prayers, inter-
cessions . . ."* (v. 1). In this chapter,
we will discuss "intercessions."

The prayers of intercession
and supplication are, of course,
prayers for others, and this scripture is talking about praying for
others.

An example of intercessory
prayer is found in Genesis 18:20-
27 where we see Abraham's intercession for the cities of Sodom and
Gomorrah.

GENESIS 18:20-27
**20 And   the   Lord   said,
Because the cry of Sodom
and Gomorrah is great, and
because their sin is very
grievous;
21 I will go down now, and
see whether they have done**

altogether according to the cry of it, which is come unto me; and if not, I will know.

22 And the men turned their faces from thence, and went toward Sodom: but Abraham stood yet before the Lord.

23 And Abraham drew near, and said, Wilt thou also destroy the righteous with the wicked?

24 Peradventure there be fifty righteous within the city: wilt thou also destroy and not spare the place for the fifty righteous that are therein?

25 That be far from thee to do after this manner, to slay the righteous with the wicked: and that the righteous should be as the wicked, that be far from thee: Shall not the Judge of all the earth do right?

26 And the Lord said, If I find in Sodom fifty righteous within the city, then I will spare all the place for their sakes.

**27 And Abraham answered
and said, Behold now, I have
taken upon me to speak
unto the Lord, which am
but dust and ashes.**

Notice that Abraham humbled
himself before the Lord, referring
to himself as *"but dust and
ashes."* It's good for us to go into
the Presence of God and get on
our face before the Lord. In many
places in the Bible we read of certain ones who laid on their faces
before the Lord. The Bible tells
us to humble ourselves, to submit
ourselves to God. *"Draw nigh to
God, and he will draw nigh to
you . . ."* (James 4:8).

I've heard people pray, "Lord,
make us humble." But He is not
going to do that. That is one
prayer that never will be
answered. He is not going to
make you humble. He tells you to
humble yourself.

When Israel dedicated Solomon's Temple, God promised He would do certain things. Even if they went into sin, when they returned to God and humbled themselves He would hear them, answer them, and restore them. *"If my people, which are called by my name, shall humble themselves, and pray, and seek my face, and turn from their wicked ways; then will I hear from heaven, and will forgive their sin, and will heal their land"* (2 Chron. 7:14). He is not going to humble you. He may permit some things to happen that will humiliate you, but He's not going to humble you. You must humble yourself.

So we see that Abraham humbled himself. There is nothing good in us, from the natural standpoint, except that Jesus dwells in us. Without Him, we are nothing, we are *"but dust and ashes"* (Gen. 18:27).

As I pray in private before I enter the pulpit to preach, I simply say, "Lord, I have no merit of my own to base any answers to prayer on. I don't come in my own name. I just throw myself on Your mercy. Without You, I am nothing."

There is an important principle, a nugget of truth, in Genesis 18. Abraham is having a conversation with God.

GENESIS 18:28-32
28 Peradventure there shall lack five of the fifty righteous: wilt thou destroy all the city for lack of five? And he [God] said, If I find there forty and five, I will not destroy it.
29 And he spake unto him yet again, and said, Peradventure there shall be forty found there. And he said, I will not do it for forty's sake.
30 And he said unto him, Oh let not the Lord be angry,

and I will speak: Peradventure there shall thirty be found there. And he said, I will not do it, if I find thirty there.

31 And he said, Behold now, I have taken upon me to speak unto the Lord: Peradventure there shall be twenty found there. And he said, I will not destroy it for twenty's sake.

32 And he said, Oh let not the Lord be angry, and I will speak yet but this once . . . .

How I wish Abraham wouldn't have said he would speak just *one* more time. I believe if he had asked, "Lord, if You can find five . . . ," the Lord would have said, "All right, if I find five righteous I won't destroy the city." I'm thoroughly convinced the Lord would have spared the city for even one. But Abraham stopped at ten. "*. . . Peradventure ten shall be found there. And he said, I will* *not destroy it for ten's sake"* (Gen. 18:32).

What a tremendous statement! "I will not destroy Sodom and Gomorrah for ten's sake." Imagine God's saying He would spare that wicked place! He had already spoken about the sexual impurity of those cities. Yet, He said He would spare them for the sake of ten righteous men.

This world certainly would be in a mess if it weren't for Christians. It already would have been destroyed if it weren't for us. No wonder Jesus said, *"Ye are the salt of the earth . . ."* (Matt. 5:13).

I can remember back before we had refrigerators or freezers when my grandmother used to can a lot of fruits and vegetables. When my grandfather killed hogs, he put salt on the meat to preserve it. Without the salt the meat would spoil and rot. This world is bad enough, but if it weren't for Christians, it certainly would be rotten. *"Ye are the salt of the earth: but if the salt have lost his savour, wherewith shall it be salted? it is thenceforth good for nothing, but to be cast out, and to be trodden under foot of men"* (Matt. 5:13). Have we lost our savour?

We can change things by prayer. We can hold back judgment even on the unsaved, and give them a little more of a chance to hear the Gospel. God told Abraham that if there were ten righteous to be found in Sodom and Gommorah, He would spare the cities.

I believe there are more than ten righteous men in America today. I believe there are people who will take their place in prayer just as Abraham did in intercession. If we will do this, we can change things. And it doesn't take a great number to do it.

Too many times we read newspaper articles and hear sermons about what the devil is doing. We hear how terrible things are. People haven't told you a thing when they tell you that. You knew it already. If you go to church and hear that kind of sermon, you go away without having eaten anything. I don't care what the devil is doing. There are some principles of prayer written in the Bible that apply to us today whereby we can change things.

Some people declare, "The Bible says that in the end time, '. . . *evil men and seducers shall wax worse and worse, deceiving, and being deceived*'" (2 Tim. 3:13). This is true. However, the people of Sodom and Gomorrah were waxing worse and worse. Yet God said for the sake of ten righteous He would not destroy the city,

because a man of God had inter-
ceded in their behalf.

Another scripture concerning
intercession is found in Ezekiel
22:30,31:

> **EZEKIEL 22:30,31**
> **30 And I sought for a man
> among them, that should
> make up the hedge, and
> stand in the gap before me
> for the land, that I should not
> destroy it: but I found none.**
> **31 Therefore have I poured
> out mine indignation upon
> them; I have consumed them
> with the fire of my wrath:
> their own way have I recom-
> pensed upon their heads,
> saith the Lord God.**

God said this concerning Israel,
yet there is a spiritual truth that
applies to us today. God said, *". . . I
sought for a man among them . . .
but I found none"* (v. 30). Isn't that
a terrible indictment? God had
told Abraham that if He found ten
righteous He would not destroy

the cities of Sodom and Gomorrah. This Scripture talks about a whole country, a whole nation. God said if He could find one righteous man He wouldn't destroy the land. *One* man could save the nation.

If God really wanted to spare the land, why didn't He just do it? Why doesn't God just do what He wants to do? In First Timothy 2:4 we read that God wills all men should come unto the knowledge of the truth. If He is Almighty, all powerful, and can do anything He wants to do, why doesn't He go ahead and save everyone?

The answer is found in the Book of Genesis. After God made the earth and the fullness thereof, He made man. He then gave Adam dominion over all the works of his hands, and Adam became the ruler of this world. However, Adam committed high treason and sold out to Satan. Then Satan became the ruler, the god of this world, and he began to dominate the earth.

In Second Corinthians 4:4 Paul calls Satan the god of this world: *"In whom the god of this world hath blinded the minds of them which believe not, lest the light of the glorious gospel of Christ, who is the image of God, should shine unto them."*

In the fourth chapter of Luke we read about the temptation of Jesus.

LUKE 4:5-7
5 And the devil, taking him up into an high mountain, shewed unto him all the kingdoms of the world in a moment of time.
6 And the devil said unto him, All this power will I give thee, and the glory of them: for that is delivered unto me; and to whomsoever I will I give it.
7 If thou therefore wilt worship me, all shall be thine.

If this were not true, Jesus would have known it. However, He didn't dispute Satan in this. He merely said, "*. . . it is written, Thou shalt worship the Lord thy God, and him only shalt thou serve*" (v. 8).

Satan offered to Jesus all the glory of the kingdoms of this world. If he had not been able to do this, then it would not have been a real temptation. And if it had not been a bona fide temptation, then the Bible would have been lying when it said Jesus was tempted of the devil. However, the glory of this world *was* Satan's to offer, for it became his when Adam sinned.

Therefore, who is responsible for the wars, murders, and violence in the world? The devil is. These don't come from God. "*Every good gift and every perfect gift is from above, and cometh down from the Father of lights, with whom is no variableness, neither shadow of turning"* (James 1:17). And God can intervene only as Christians seek His face and ask Him to move: *". . . ye have not, because ye ask not"* (James 4:2).

Satan's authority over matters on the earth can only be overcome as Christians pray and intercede in behalf of our country. God is looking today for someone who will *". . . make up the hedge, and stand in the gap before me for the land, that I should not destroy it . . ."* (Ezek. 22:30).

Chapter 2
Dealing With Strongholds

In the Book of Daniel, we read a passage of Scripture concerning intercession that will be a tremendous challenge to our prayer life if we fully grasp it.

DANIEL 10:2,3
2 In those days I Daniel was mourning [fasting] **three full weeks.**
3 I ate no pleasant bread, neither came flesh nor wine in my mouth, neither did I anoint myself at all, till three whole weeks were fulfilled.

This Scripture makes it clear there are different ways to fast. Fasting doesn't always mean total abstinence from food. Notice

Daniel said, *"I ate no pleasant bread . . . ."*

DANIEL 10:10-13

10 And, behold, an hand touched me [Daniel], which set me upon my knees and upon the palms of my hands.

11 And he [God] said unto me, O Daniel, a man greatly beloved, understand the words that I speak unto thee, and stand upright: for unto thee am I now sent. And when he had spoken this word unto me, I stood trembling.

12 Then said he unto me, Fear not, Daniel: for from the first day that thou didst set thine heart to understand, and to chasten thyself before thy God, thy words were heard, and I am come for thy words.

13 But the prince of the kingdom of Persia withstood me one and twenty days: but, lo, Michael, one of the chief princes, came to help me;

**and I remained there with
the kings of Persia.**

Notice first of all that the
angel was not sent from heaven
to Daniel with the message until
Daniel prayed. God sent the
answer on the first day. But the
answer was twenty-one days in
getting there. Sometimes when
we pray, the answer doesn't get
through instantly. That doesn't
mean God doesn't hear us or hasn't
sent the answer. He has sent it,
but it doesn't get through. Verse
13 explains that the prince of
Persia withstood the angel.

The Bible is not talking here
about a physical person. An
angel is not a physical being; he
is a spiritual being. In other
words, there was on the earth an
earthly kingdom with a prince of
Persia heading it up. But right
above it in the heavenlies was a
spiritual kingdom. In that kingdom was a prince of Persia who

really dominated the government of Persia. He didn't want the angel to get through with the answer. The message the angel brought concerning Israel was that this Medo-Persian kingdom would be dissolved, the Grecian kingdom would come, and finally the Roman kingdom would come and rule over Jerusalem.

When the prince of Persia withstood the angel, God sent another angel, and finally, on the twenty-first day, he got through to Daniel with the message. Notice what the angel said as he left him: "*. . . now will I return to fight with the prince of Persia: and when I am gone forth, lo, the prince of Grecia* [Greece] *shall come*" (Dan. 10:20).

In Ephesians 6:12 we read, "*For we wrestle not against flesh and blood, but against principalities, against powers, against the rulers of the darkness of this*

*world, against spiritual wicked-
ness* [wicked spirits] *in high
places."*

There are three heavens spoken of in the Bible: the heaven of
heavens where God's throne is,
the heaven above us where the
planets and stars are, and the
atmospheric heaven right above
us. The atmospheric heaven is
the one this scripture refers to.

In this unseen world Satan has
the authority. He is ruling. That
should be obvious to anyone. I was
amused some time ago while read-
ing an article by a columnist. He
didn't claim to be a Christian.
However, he didn't claim to be an
atheist either.

He said, "Maybe you would
call me an agnostic. An agnostic
says, 'If there is a God, I don't
know it.' Yet I don't really classify
myself as an agnostic because I
believe there is a God. But I can't
go along with what a lot of people,

even Christians, say about God. I've heard preachers say God is running everything. However, if He is, He's sure got things in a mess!"

That columnist has a point. If God is running everything, He does have things in a mess.

However, Satan set up his kingdom here on the earth in the spirit realm when Adam sold out to him. He set up the powers, the principalities, and the rulers of darkness of this world that we have to deal with. And this is where we wrestle in making intercession. It's not with God. God is not withholding from us.

The scripture says, ". . . *We wrestle not against flesh and blood . . . ,*" but we do have to wrestle. It doesn't just say, ". . . *We wrestle not*" and stop there. It says ". . . *We wrestle not against flesh and blood, but against principalities, against powers, against the rulers of the darkness of this world . . ."* (Eph. 6:12).

As Christians, we simply have to stand our ground, know what belongs to us, and refuse to be moved. Those who expect to float through life on flowery beds of ease are mistaken.

I am appalled at Christians who say, "Why did this happen to me?" Some people act like they are the only ones that things happen to. But the devil will throw every roadblock he can in the Christian's way.

Instead of spending all your time trying to figure out why a certain thing happened, stand up, look the devil right in the face, and say, "Mr. Devil, I believe God, that it shall be even as it was told me in God's Word! You are not going to dominate me!"

That's the reason Paul told the Church at Ephesus, *"Neither give place to the devil"* (Eph. 4:27). He will take a place in you if you will let him, but you have authority over him.

In Ezekiel 28, we see more about this double kingdom — the natural kingdom upon the earth and the spiritual kingdom.

EZEKIEL 28:1,2
1 The word of the Lord came again unto me, saying,
2 Son of man, say unto the prince of Tyrus, Thus saith the Lord God; Because thine heart is lifted up, and thou hast said, I am a God, I sit in the seat of God, in the midst of the seas; yet thou art a MAN, and not God, though thou set thine heart as the heart of God.

The prince of Tyrus referred to here is a man, for the Lord said, "Yet thou art a *man.*"

Then beginning with the verse eleven we read:

EZEKIEL 28:11-17

11 Moreover the word of the Lord came unto me, saying,

12 Son of man, take up a lamentation upon the king of Tyrus, and say unto him, Thus saith the Lord God; Thou sealest up the sum, full of wisdom, and perfect in beauty.

13 Thou hast been in Eden the garden of God; every precious stone was thy covering, the sardius, topaz, and the diamond, the beryl, the onyx, and the jasper, the sapphire, the emerald, and the carbuncle, and gold: the workmanship of thy tabrets and of thy pipes was prepared in thee in the day that thou wast created.

14 Thou art the anointed cherub that covereth; and I have set thee so: thou wast upon the holy mountain of God; thou hast walked up and down in the midst of the stones of fire.

15 Thou wast perfect in thy ways from the day that thou wast created, till iniquity was found in thee.

16 By the multitude of thy merchandise they have filled the midst of thee with violence, and thou hast sinned: therefore I will cast thee as profane out of the mountain of God: and I will destroy thee, O covering cherub, from the midst of the stones of fire.

17 Thine heart was lifted up because of thy beauty, thou hast corrupted thy wisdom by reason of thy brightness: I will cast thee to the ground, I will lay thee before kings, that they may behold thee.

It is quite obvious here that God is not talking about a man. He is talking about a spirit being. At first HE speaks of the prince of Tyrus, saying to him, *". . . yet thou art a man. . . ."*

But when He spoke to the king of Tyrus He said, *"Thou hast been in Eden the garden of God. . . ."* The prince of Tyrus was not there; but Satan was. The Bible here is talking about Satan, or Lucifer. It is saying that on earth the prince of Tyrus had an earthly kingdom he ruled over, but that an invisible kingdom was behind it. Satan with his invisible kingdom was actually ruling. So we see this double kingdom reference both in this scripture in Ezekiel and in our scripture in the Book of Daniel.

In Second Corinthians 10:4 and 5 we read:

2 CORINTHIANS 10:4,5
4 (For the weapons of our warfare are not carnal, but mighty through God to the pulling down of strong holds;)
5 Casting down imagina-tions, and every high thing that exalteth itself against the knowledge of God, and bringing into captivity

every thought to the obedience of Christ.

In this spiritual war, we do have weapons, but they are not guns or grenades. Our weapons "*. . . are not carnal, but are mighty through God to the pulling down of strong holds.*" The powers opposing us are satanic strongholds; powers in the realm of darkness. This is where prayer comes in.

I held a revival in a church for a pastor whom I knew, loved, and respected. The people in the church were wonderful people, loved their pastor, loved me, and were receptive to the preaching of the Word. But this was the hardest place I had ever preached in my life. Every word seemed to bounce right back at me off the walls.

In the process of time, while I was between meetings, I was

called upon to preach in that church again. It was the same crowd, but there was a marked difference. There was as much difference as between daylight and dark.

After the service the new pastor asked if I could see any difference in the church. "Was it any easier to preach tonight than it was before?"

"Why, there is no comparison," I answered. "Everything was so free and easy tonight, whereas before it seemed bound and tight — spiritually dead. What happened?"

"I'd been here for months," the pastor said, "and finally I decided I was tired of that dead spirit. I determined I was going to break through it. I set myself to fast and pray for that one thing.

"On the seventh day of the fast, while praying, I had a vision, and before my eyes I saw the ceiling above the pulpit disappear. Sitting above the ceiling on a rafter was a spirit that looked like a big ape or baboon. God was showing me there was a spirit power right above the natural that was holding things back.

"I spoke to the spirit and commanded him to come down. He didn't say a word, but I could tell he didn't want to. Reluctantly, he came down. Then I said, 'Not only must you come down from there, but you must get out of here,' and I pointed up at the aisle of the church. He started up the aisle, and I followed him. He would take a few steps and turn around, almost like a little dog with an expression that said, 'Do I have to leave? Can I come back?'

"When he would pause, I would say, 'No, get out of here,' and I followed him to the front door of the church. There he paused once again. I kept commanding him to go out and finally he walked on down the street and disappeared into a nightclub."

Sometimes in dealing with people as well as with churches, I have dealt with the spirit behind the person. Often in prayer God will show you how to do it, just as He did with this pastor. But if we don't know anything about spiritual praying, we are at a disadvantage.

Many times we blame things on *people* when there is a *power* behind the whole situation. We try to deal with the *people*. Sometimes a preacher will get up and beat the people over the head when it is the power behind the thing that needs to be dealt with.

Who is going to deal with these satanic forces? God? No. Second Corinthians 10:4 and 5 says these are the weapons of *our* warfare, not God's warfare. Our weapons are not carnal, but they are mighty through God. He has provided the weapons for us to pull down the strongholds. If we don't do it, they never will be pulled down.

When Daniel was interceding for Israel, he set his face to seek God. The angel came and said:

DANIEL 10:13,14
13 But the prince of the kingdom of Persia withstood me one and twenty days: but, lo, Michael, one of the chief princes, came to help me; and I remained there with the kings of Persia.
14 Now I am come to make thee understand what shall befall thy people in the latter days: for yet the vision is for many days.

The angel brought the answer. He came through with it. But the key was Daniel. The key wasn't God. The key wasn't the angel. The key wasn't the prince of Persia. The key to the whole situation was Daniel. He was the man who brought things to pass through persevering prayer.

Chapter 3
Praying With
the Help
of the Holy Spirit

Likewise the Spirit also helpeth our infirmities: for we know not what we should pray for as we ought: but the Spirit itself maketh intercession for us with groanings which cannot be uttered.

And he that searcheth the hearts knoweth what is the mind of the Spirit, because he maketh intercession for the saints according to the will of God.

— Romans 8:26,27

In the above scriptures, Paul says, *"for we know not what we should pray for as we ought. . . ."* From our study in chapter 1, we know we should pray for

". . . *kings, and for all that are in authority*" (1 Tim. 2:2); that is, the rulers of our nation. The Spirit will help us pray according to the will of God.

In First Corinthians 14 Paul says:

1 CORINTHIANS 14:14,15
14 For if I pray in an unknown tongue, my spirit prayeth, but my understanding is unfruitful.
15 What is it then? I will pray with the [my] spirit, and I will pray with the [my] understanding also: I will sing with the [my] spirit, and I will sing with the [my] understanding also.

When Paul speaks here about our understanding, he is referring to our minds. He is talking about two kinds of praying: *mental* praying and *spiritual* praying. There is a difference between the two.

People usually think all praying is spiritual, but it isn't. Therefore Paul said, *"If I pray in an unknown tongue, my spirit prayeth . . ."* (v. 14). He was praying with his spirit. If he had prayed with his understanding, he would have been praying from his mind.

God wants us to pray in the Spirit, but He also wants us to pray with our understanding. That is why Paul said, *". . . I will pray with the spirit, and I will pray with the understanding also . . ."* (v. 15). In *The Amplified Bible* we are told, "For if I pray in an [unknown] tongue, my spirit [by the Holy Spirit within me] prays . . ." (v. 14). When you pray in tongues, it is the Holy Spirit within you giving you the utterance, but it is *your* spirit doing the praying.

Mental praying — praying with your understanding — is

limited to your knowledge, to your understanding. We can see why it would be insufficient. The Church, generally speaking, has failed because for the most part it has endeavored to carry on the work of God with only one kind of praying: mental praying.

"Likewise the Spirit also helpeth our infirmities: for we know not what we should pray for as we ought" (Rom. 8:26). It would be impossible for us in our human reasoning to know what to pray for as we ought. Of course, I would know about things that concern me. But praying for our own individual needs is limited praying, and that is as far as many people ever go.

". . . The Spirit itself maketh intercession for us with groanings which cannot be uttered" (Rom. 8:26). According to the late P. C. Nelson, the literal Greek translation indicates, "groanings

which cannot be uttered in articulate speech." Articulate speech means our ordinary speech. This verse is referring to praying with tongues, for Paul is telling the Corinthians and the Romans the same thing. In other words, those groanings that well up inside us while we are in prayer come out of our spirit. They cannot be put into regular speech.

This isn't something the Holy Spirit does apart from you. It is something the Holy Spirit helps you to do. The Holy Spirit wasn't sent to the earth to do anything by Himself apart from the Church. He was sent to empower us to do things. In John 14:16 Jesus said, *". . . I will pray the Father, and he shall give you another Comforter . . . ."* In many translations this scripture reads, "I will send you another Helper" rather than Comforter.

The helper on any job is not the one *responsible* for the job. He's there to *help* the one who is supposed to do the job. *The Holy Spirit is not going to do your praying for you*. These groanings are not the Holy Spirit's groanings, but groanings which cannot be uttered in articulate speech. They are groanings that come from within your innermost being and escape your lips in prayer. That is the Spirit helping you to pray.

That agrees exactly with what Paul says: *"For if I pray in an unknown tongue, my spirit* [by the Holy Spirit within me] *prayeth . . ."* (1 Cor. 14:14). Groaning in prayer and speaking with tongues is the Holy Spirit helping us to pray. One of the mightiest weapons to be used in prayer is praying in tongues.

In connection with this, notice something else concerning spiritual travail and prayer: the two are related. Writing to all the churches throughout Galatia, Paul said, *"My little children, of whom I travail in birth again until Christ be formed in you"* (Gal. 4:19). Paul already had travailed for them to be birthed, but he continued to pray for them in the Spirit for their spiritual growth. They had been born again. They were even filled with the Spirit. But Christ had not been formed in them as He should. They had not grown in grace. Instead of going forward in Christ, they had wanted to get back under the law.

In Isaiah 66:8 and 9 we read:

ISAIAH 66:8,9
8 Who hath heard such a thing? who hath seen such things? Shall the earth be made to bring forth in one day? or shall a nation be born at once? for as soon as Zion travailed, she brought forth her children.

**9   Shall I bring to the birth,
and not cause to bring forth?
saith the LORD: shall I cause
to bring forth, and shut the
womb? saith thy God.**

Many think these scriptures
just refer to the rebirth and
rebuilding of Israel as a nation as
we have seen it. However, Isaiah
was prophesying about something different, as we shall see in
the next scripture.

Writing to the Hebrew Christians, Paul said:

HEBREWS 12:18-21
18 For ye [the Hebrew
[Christians] **are not come
unto the mount** [referring to
Mount Sinai where the law was
given to Moses] **that might be
touched, and that burned
with fire, nor unto blackness,
and darkness, and tempest,
19 And the sound of a trum-
pet, and the voice of words;
which voice they that heard
intreated that the word**

**should not be spoken to
them any more:
20 (For they could not
endure that which was
commanded, And if so much
as a beast touch the mountain, it shall be stoned, or
thrust through with a dart:
21 And so terrible was the
sight, that Moses said, I
exceedingly   fear   and
quake:).**

These verses refer to Mount
Sinai where the law was given;
they concern Israel. Yet to the
Hebrew Christians who had
become born-again believers,
Paul said, *"But ye are come unto
Mount Sion"* (Heb. 12:22). He
was telling them, "You are not
come to Mount Sinai. You are
come to Mount Zion."

And of Mount Zion he says:

**HEBREWS 12:22-24
22** [You are come] **. . . unto the
city of the living God, the
heavenly Jerusalem, and to**

**an innumerable company of
angels,
23 To the general assembly
and church of the firstborn,
which are written in
heaven, and to God the
Judge of all, and to the spir-
its of just men made per-
fect,
24 And to Jesus the media-
tor of the new covenant,
and to the blood of sprin-
kling, that speaketh better
things than that of Abel.**

Therefore, we see that when
Isaiah was prophesying about
Mount Zion, he was talking
about all who believe in Christ.

With that thought in mind,
let us refer again to our Scripture in Isaiah, for it will take on
a new significance.

**ISAIAH 66: 8,9
8 . . . for as soon as Zion
travailed, she brought forth
her children.**

9 Shall I bring to the birth, and not cause to bring forth? saith the LORD: shall I cause to bring forth, and shut the womb? saith thy God.

Paul, writing to the churches in Galatia, said, "My little children, of whom I travail in birth again . . ." (Gal. 4:19). This meant that he had travailed for them at one time in birth. Now he travailed that Christ might be formed in them.

In light of the passages of Scripture we have just studied, the verses in Romans 8:26 and 27 will take on new significance.

ROMANS 8:26,27
26 Likewise the Spirit also helpeth our infirmities: for we know not what we should pray for as we ought: but the Spirit itself maketh intercession for us with groanings which cannot be uttered.

27 And he that searcheth the hearts knoweth what is the mind of the Spirit, because he maketh intercession for the saints according to the will of God.

When a woman gives birth to a child (an illustration which both Isaiah and Paul used) she travails in birth. She groans. The reason that too few people are being saved and that a lot of conversions never amount to anything is that God doesn't want conversions; He wants births. As soon as Zion travailed, she brought forth her children. *If there is no travail, there are no children.*

Do we know anything about travail, groanings? Some of us know a little about it. But many know nothing. In some churches if believers would begin to groan and cry at the altar, it would disturb people. They would say, "We're not going to have any of that around here." Then they are not going to have any births, either.

Some of the greatest things that have happened to me in my ministry came as I prayed this way with spiritual intercession. It will work now just as it did in days past. God's Word doesn't change. And just as surely as we travail in prayer, we will give birth to babes in Christ.

Now we can also make intercession for the saints in this way. Remember Paul told the Galatians, *"My little children, of whom I travail in birth again until Christ be formed in you"* (Gal. 4:19). In other words, he travailed in prayer for them until they grew up to be stalwart Christians rather than baby Christians.

In a meeting I was holding in Dallas, Texas, a young woman came forward and gave her heart to the Lord. She had a glorious experience, but in a short time she fell away from the church and I later heard she was backslidden. When I heard that, something on the inside of me seemed to say, "The church is responsible."

At the time I didn't understand how the church could be responsible for the girl's backsliding. However, later as this scripture was made real to me, I saw how the church was responsible to ". . . travail in birth again until Christ be formed . . ." (v. 19) in this new convert. Until Christ has been formed in the new believer, he will naturally keep doing some things that are wrong, even though he has been saved and filled with the Holy Spirit.

The Bible teaches there is a similarity between spiritual growth and physical growth. No one is born a full-grown human. We are born babies and we grow up. Neither is one born a full-grown Christian. He is born a baby and then grows up. As ministers and teachers we are responsible to teach new Christians. Peter said, *"As newborn babes, desire the sincere milk of the word, that ye may grow thereby"* (1 Peter 2:2).

On the other hand, the Word of God teaches that we must pray for baby Christians. Paul taught the Galatians and prayed for them too. His letter to them was full of teaching and instruction. But he also said there must be prayer — travail — for them.

While holding a revival in a small church in Oklahoma in 1950, I told the people one night that the Lord had impressed me to tell them something. I told them that if they, as believers, would give themselves to spiritual travail and intercessory prayer, they would take that town for Christ. At that time their Sunday school attendance was about 135.

A few men and women in that congregation took that to heart and began to give themselves to interceding — groaning and praying for that town as they were moved upon by the Holy Spirit.

Less than two years later I returned to that church to see a dramatic change. Originally, the members had met in an old frame building. But now they had the only brick church in town. They were located right downtown, across the street from the bank. They had a two-story Sunday school annex, an auditorium that would seat 500-600 people comfortably, and they were averaging 400 in Sunday school. Theirs was the largest church in town, and this was accomplished by prayer.

Sometimes you can do things with a church program, but that doesn't necessarily mean you are bringing people to birth. We can have all kinds of programs to get people to church, but that doesn't mean we will get them saved. We can get them to join the church, but that doesn't mean they are born again.

I know from experience that when I have a burden of prayer for a lost person, I feel the same as they do. I am taking their place. I feel that same burden of sin on my own conscience, it seems.

People have said to me, "I know I'm saved. I'm filled with the Holy Spirit, and I'm walking in all the light I have. But many times when the altar call is given, such a burden comes on me I feel as if I'm lost. I don't understand."

They never have been taught along these lines. I tell them to sit quietly during the altar call when they feel such a burden, and to make intercession for the lost. God is wanting them to intercede for the unsaved. Because certain people have been young in spiritual things, the devil has made them believe in their natural mind that perhaps they weren't saved. They could not understand why they had such an overwhelming feeling at times.

We need more of this kind of praying, and when we have it we will get more people saved; for when Zion travailed, she brought forth children. Therefore, don't draw back if the Holy Spirit moves upon you in groanings; respond to Him.

With this kind of praying we don't need all the elaborate methods used by some churches to attract people. Some put every kind of program imaginable and use numerous gimmicks, thinking this is the way to reach people. They use every kind of weapon except spiritual weapons.

Charles G. Finney stands out as one of the greatest exponents of evangelism since the days of the Apostle Paul. All theologians and church historians agree that Finney had the greatest success of any individual preacher since the days of Paul. Furthermore, in Finney's revivals eighty percent of all his converts stayed saved.

In no other revival since the days of Paul has this been true. Moody was mightily used of God. Yet church historians agree that not more than fifty percent of his converts remained.

Since the turn of the century we have seen a great revival in the Pentecostal movement. Yet Pentecostal leaders, both past and present, agree that not even fifty percent of the converts remain true to God. No one has had the success Finney had. Yet he never used any kind of gimmick. He didn't rely on sensationalism; he depended solely upon prayer.

In his autobiography we read that when Finney would go into a town for a revival, almost the entire town would turn to God. After one such revival in which practically the entire city was converted, the only theater in town had to close down because no one attended. All the "grog" shops, Finney's term for what we know today as beer joints or nightclubs, also had to close down after the revival.

What was the secret of Finney's success? He said, "There is no more secret, no more mystery to having a revival than there is to a farmer's reaping a crop. If the farmer tills the soil, puts the seed in the ground, and trusts God for the rain, then when the time comes there will be a harvest."

Finney had an elderly man working with him who was semi-retired from the ministry. People called him "Father Nash." Father Nash would go ahead of Finney three weeks in advance of a planned revival to try to get two or three people to enter into a covenant of prayer with him. Someone asked Finney what kind of man this Father Nash was. "We never see him," they said. "He doesn't enter into any of the meetings."

Finney replied, "Like anybody who does a lot of praying, Father Nash is a very quiet person."

Show me a person who is always talking and I'll show you a Christian who never does much praying.

"On one occasion when I got to a town to start a revival," Finney said, "a lady who ran a boarding house contacted me. She said, 'Brother Finney, do you know a Father Nash? He and two other men have been at my boarding house for the last three days, but they haven't eaten a bite of food. I opened the door and peeped in at them because I could hear them groaning, and I saw them drum on their faces. They have been this way for three days, lying prostrate on the floor and groaning. I thought something awful must have happened to them. I was afraid to go in and I didn't know what to do.

Would you please come see about them?'

"'No, it isn't necessary,' I replied. 'They just have a spirit of travail in prayer.'"

Finney prayed much himself. Rising every morning at 4 o'clock, he would go out into the country and pray until 8 o'clock.

As we look again at the scriptures in Romans 8:26 and 27 in a little more detail, we see how they also relate to travail in prayer on the behalf of others. There are some who will be saved because they hear the truth and respond to it. *But there are others who never will be saved unless somebody intercedes for them.* Only intercessory prayer will break the power of the devil over them and release them.

There are people who will be healed by simply believing what God's Word has to say on the sub-

ject and by appropriating healing unto themselves. This is
what I did when I was raised up
from what doctors said was my
deathbed. Some will be healed by
the laying on of hands and
anointing with oil. But some
such as unsaved people or baby
Christians who don't know their
rights in Christ will never be
healed by any of these methods.
Somebody will have to pray for
them.

Prayer and travail on the
behalf of others works. These
other things, such as laying on of
hands, require the individual's
direct cooperation. But prevailing
prayer overpowers the works of
the devil — "*. . . to the pulling
down of strong holds*" (2 Cor. 10:4).

A Presbyterian pastor told me
about a member of his church —
a young mother with three children — who had open heart
surgery. During such an opera-

tion it is necessary to stop the heartbeat, of course. However, after they started it again, the woman died. The doctors managed to get her heart going again, but they said there was absolutely no chance for the young woman to live.

Even if she were to revive, it would have been better for her to die, for her brain had been deprived of too much oxygen. If she were to live, she probably would not know anything. It was inevitable that she had brain damage.

During that night while the pastor was sleeping, he was awakened by the sound of someone groaning. He noticed his wife wasn't in bed, so he supposed she must have become ill. He got up to see about her, and found her on her face on the living room floor, groaning and praying in tongues. As they were new in the things of the Spirit, he didn't understand what was happening, nor did his wife.

He asked, "Honey, what is the matter?"

"I don't understand it," she said, "but in my spirit I have a burden to pray for the girl who had heart surgery. I just can't let her die."

"Maybe we shouldn't pray that she would live," he said. "If she lives, her mind won't be right, and that will be a terrible thing for those three children."

The wife replied that even though she couldn't understand it, she had this overwhelming burden and had to pray for the young woman. She spent three nights in prayer, groaning and praying in tongues.

On the fourth day the young mother suddenly regained consciousness and was completely healed. Her mind was keen and alert. The doctors were astonished. This remarkable healing came about because the Spirit helped the pastor's wife in prayer.

In Romans 8:26 we also see a truth regarding healing for ourselves. "Likewise the Spirit also helpeth our infirmities . . . ." In Matthew 8:17 we read, ". . . *Himself* [Jesus] *took our infirmities, and bare our sicknesses.*" We know that Jesus purchased healing for us, but it is the Holy Spirit who brings that healing to our bodies. He is the agency.

In studying this portion of Scripture in the Greek, we learn that there are actually three Greek words involved in the English word that is translated "helpeth." One of the Greek words means "to take hold together." Another Greek word means "with." The third Greek word means "against." The three together, then, mean "to take hold together with against."

Therefore, Romans 8:26 means that the Spirit "takes hold together with us against our infirmities." This implies that if we don't take a stand, the Spirit doesn't have anything to take hold with us against.

The next clause in Romans 8:26 says, ". . . *for we know not what we should pray for as we ought. . .*" This implies that we take hold together with the Spirit against our infirmities in praying in the Spirit.

We can see, then, that the reason some do not receive healing is that they do not take a stand against their infirmity of sickness. The Holy Spirit doesn't have anything to "take hold with them against." If He doesn't have their cooperation in prayer, He has no one with whom He can "take hold with against," He has no way in which to bring healing.

Another interesting thing to note about Romans 8:26, *"Like-wise the Spirit also helpeth our infirmities . . ."* is the word "also." This means that the Spirit helps too. Jesus did something about our infirmities. *"Himself took our infirmities, and bare our sick-nesses"* (Matt. 8:17), but *". . . the Spirit also helpeth our infirmi-ties . . ."*

Sometimes when problems arise which involve me, my fam-ily, or friends, I get on my knees and say, "Lord, I don't know how to pray about this; I don't know how to pray as I ought. But You know, and Your Word says the Holy Spirit is to be my Helper. I trust and believe You to help me."

Then I begin to pray in other tongues. Sometimes I start out to pray within myself without any particular anointing. As Smith Wigglesworth said, "I start out in the flesh and wind up in the Spirit."

Some people are waiting for the Holy Spirit to make them do something. They are waiting for something to overpower them. However, we don't need to wait for some special feeling. We can just know that the Helper is there, and we can ask Him to help us. Then as we believe He is helping us, He will "take hold together with us against" that problem.

A Sinner's Prayer To Receive Jesus as Savior

Dear Heavenly Father,

I come to You in the Name of Jesus.

Your Word says, "...*him that cometh to me I will in no wise cast out*" (John 6:37),

So I know You won't cast me out, but You take me in,

And I thank You for it.

You said in Your Word, "*Whosoever shall call upon the name of the Lord shall be saved*" (Rom. 10:13).

I am calling on Your name,

So I know You have saved me now.

You also said, ". . . *if thou shalt confess with thy mouth the Lord Jesus, and shalt believe in thine heart that God hath raised him from the dead, thou shalt be saved. For with the heart man believeth unto righteousness; and*

*with the mouth confession is
made unto salvation"*
(Rom. 10:9,10).

I believe in my heart that Jesus
Christ is the Son of God.

I believe that He was raised from
the dead for my justification.

And I confess Him now as my Lord,

Because Your Word says, "*. . .with
the heart man believeth unto
righteousness. . .*" and I do believe
with my heart,

I have now become the righteousness of God in Christ
(2 Cor. 5:21),

And I am saved!

Thank You, Lord!

Signed _____

Date _____

About the Author

The ministry of Kenneth E. Hagin has spanned more than 60 years since God miraculously healed him of a deformed heart and incurable blood disease at the age of 17. Today the scope of Kenneth Hagin Ministries is worldwide. The ministry's radio program, "Faith Seminar of the Air," is heard coast to coast in the U.S. and reaches more than 100 nations. Other outreaches include: *The Word of Faith*, a free monthly magazine; crusades, conducted nationwide; RHEMA Correspondence Bible School; RHEMA Bible Training Center; RHEMA Alumni Association and RHEMA Ministerial Association International; and a prison outreach.